SCHIRMER PERFORMANCE EDITIONS

# BAROQUE TO MODERN

## Early Intermediate Level

29 Pieces by 20 Composers in Progressive Order

Compiled and Edited by Richard Walters

*On the cover:*
Detail from *St. Cecilia* (1606)
by Guido Reni (1575–1642)

Detail from *Jeanne Hebuterne, sitzend* (1918)
by Amedeo Modigliani (1884–1920)

ISBN 978-1-4950-8861-2

## G. SCHIRMER, *Inc.*

DISTRIBUTED BY
HAL•LEONARD®
7777 W. BLUEMOUND RD. P.O. BOX 13819 MILWAUKEE, WI 53213

www.musicsalesclassical.com
**www.halleonard.com**

# CONTENTS

Though the table of contents appears in alphabetical order
by composer, the music in this book is in progressive order.

# COMPOSER BIOGRAPHIES, HISTORICAL NOTES
## AND
# PRACTICE AND PERFORMANCE TIPS

## ANONYMOUS
(Baroque Era)

Johann Sebastian Bach included the following pieces (BWV Appendix 116 and 126) in the second volume, dated 1725, of the *Notebook for Anna Magdalena Bach*. The notebooks (the first was begun in 1722) were for Bach's second wife, Anna Magdalena, who was much younger than the composer. Such keyboard notebooks of assembled favorite pieces were common in Baroque homes, and used for family music-making. Some of the pieces in the Anna Magdalena notebook are by J.S. Bach; others are not. Previously attributed to Bach, we now know that the pieces below are not J.S. Bach compositions. The composers are unknown. We can assume that they date from the first decades of the eighteenth century and are likely German in origin.

### Minuet in G Major, BWV Appendix 116
*Practice and Performance Tips*
- Note that the tempo, articulations and dynamics are editorial suggestions, since the composer did not provide these, which is common in this period.
- First practice hands separately, beginning at a slow tempo.
- Then practice hands together at a slow tempo.
- The repeated quarter notes in the right hand in measures 2, 4, 5, 10 and 12 should be played with slight separation.
- The quarter notes of the left hand throughout should be played slightly detached.
- Aim for steadiness and graceful gentleness, common in a minuet.
- Your final performance tempo should not be too fast.
- Use no sustaining pedal.

### Musette in D Major, BWV Appendix 126
A musette was a small French bagpipe in the seventeenth and eighteenth centuries. A musical piece called a musette is dance music with a melody idiomatic for the musette (imagine an oboe playing the melody line), over a bass line drone.

*Practice and Performance Tips*
- Note that the tempo, articulations and dynamics are editorial suggestions, since the composer did not provide these, which is common in this period.
- First practice hands separately, beginning at a slow tempo.
- Then practice hands together at a slow tempo.
- To find Baroque style, play any notes not marked with slurs as slightly detached. This applies to all the eighth notes of the left hand, and the eighth notes of the right hand in measures 3–4, 7–8, 10–11, 18–19, 23–24, and 27–28.
- Note the editorial suggestion of "Moderato." Some students play this musette too quickly.
- A very slight slowing down might be applied to the final bar.
- Use no sustaining pedal.

## BÉLA BARTÓK
(1881–1945, Hungarian;
became a US citizen in 1945)

Béla Bartók is one of the most important and often performed composers of the twentieth century, and much of his music, including *Concerto for Orchestra*, his concertos, his string quartets, and his opera *Bluebeard's Castle*, holds a venerable position in the classical repertoire. His parents were amateur musicians who nurtured their young son with exposure to dance music, drumming, and piano lessons. In 1899 he started piano and composition studies at the Academy of Music in Budapest and not long after graduation he joined the Academy's piano faculty. Bartók wished to create music that was truly Hungarian at its core, a desire that sparked his deep interest in folk music. His work collecting and studying folksongs from around the Baltic region impacted his own compositional style greatly in terms of rhythm, mood, and texture. Bartók utilized folk influences to create a truly unique style. Though he composed opera, concertos, ballets, and chamber music, he was also committed to music education and composed several piano works for students, including his method *Mikrokosmos*. Bartók toured extensively in the 1920s and '30s, and became as well-known as both a pianist and composer. He immigrated to the US in 1940 to escape war and political turmoil in Europe, and settled in New York City, though the last years of his life were difficult, with many health problems.

### Slovak Peasant Dance from *Ten Easy Pieces*
(composed 1908)

Bartók collected and documented thousands of folksongs from Hungary and neighboring countries, which influenced his own compositions. Bartók made "art music" settings of folksongs, and also created compositions that are in the spirit of folk music. The composer didn't necessarily document which pieces were based on folksongs and which are original compositions in that style.

*Practice and Performance Tips*
- Learn the composer's articulation from the beginning, as you learn the notes and rhythms.
- First practice hands separately.
- As the music is mastered, increase practice speed, but always maintain steadiness at any tempo.
- Quiet, crisp *staccato* playing predominates.
- Carefully note which notes are marked with a tenuto, and which are marked *staccato*.
- At *poco sostenuto* (a little more sustained) in measure 42, a very slight *rit.* is possible.
- Use no sustaining pedal.

## LUDWIG VAN BEETHOVEN
(1770–1827, German)

Beethoven was the major figure of the transition from the Classical Era to the Romantic Era in music. As one of the first successful freelance composers, as opposed to a composer thriving in a royal court appointment, Beethoven wrote widely in nearly every genre of his day, with emphasis on instrumental music. He acquired wealth and fame beyond any composer before him. Beethoven's chamber music, piano sonatas, concertos, and symphonies are part of the ever-present international repertoire. In his youth he was regarded as one of the greatest pianists of his time, but he stopped performing after hearing loss set in. He devoted an enormous amount of his compositional efforts to the piano, which as an instrument came of age during his lifetime. He was occasionally a piano teacher, with wealthy patrons and young prodigies begging for lessons, though this task was not a match for his nature. However, teaching piano did inspire him to write many pieces for students. Because his piano music is so widely spread across the level of difficulty from easy to virtuoso, Beethoven's piano music is played by students and professional pianists.

### Sonatina in G Major, Kinsky-Halm Anh. 5, No. 1
(attributed to Beethoven)

Scholars now believe this sonatina likely is not by Beethoven, but another composer that has not been identified.

*Practice and Performance Tips*
- A key component of Classical style at the keyboard is an accompaniment figure called the Alberti Bass, such as in the left hand in measures 5–6 and 21–22 of the first movement. This needs to be played very evenly.
- The composer has provided a few clues about articulation, and we have added other editorial suggestions appropriate to this style.
- Carefully pay attention to the two-note slurs in measures 2, 7, 18, and 23 of the first movement.
- Play the quarter notes of the left hand in measures 7, 23 and 32–33 slightly detached in the first movement.
- The second movement is a "Romanza," which is indication of a songlike spirit.
- Note that in this Classical style, the grace notes in measures 30 and 34 begin on the beat.
- Notice how in measures 1 and 2 in the left hand, the lower note is an eighth note, but in measures 3 and 4, the lower note is sustained.
- Probably use no sustaining pedal throughout.

## JOHANN FRIEDRICH BURGMÜLLER
(1806–1874, German/French)

The Burgmüllers were a musical family. Johann August Franz, the patriarch, was a composer and theatre music director as well as the founder of the

Lower Rhine Music Festival. Johann Friedrich's brother Norbert was a child prodigy at the piano and a composer. Johann Freidrich distinguished himself from his family by leaving Germany and establishing a career in Parisian circles as a composer of French salon music. Later in life he withdrew from performing and focused on teaching. He wrote many short character pieces for his students as etudes. Several collections of these are perennial favorites of piano teachers, especially opuses 100, 105, and 109.

### Sincerity (La Candeur) from *25 Easy and Progressive Studies*, Op. 100, No. 1

The original French title of the set from 1852 is *25 Études faciles et progressives*.

*Practice and Performance Tips*
- This piece is primarily about flowing, even eighth notes.
- Note the difference between the four-note slurs and the eight-note slurs. The harmony becomes colorful and surprising in measure 13 in the B section briefly before resolving back to the tonic key.
- The title of the piece, "La Candeur" (Sincerity), is an indication not to take this music too rapidly. We suggest that the composer intends a purity of spirit.
- Sustaining pedal may be used, but the piece could also be played without it. A change of harmony is a clue as to where to change the pedal.
- As with all of Burgmüller's short pieces, pay careful attention to the many details of dynamics and articulation.

### Ballade from *25 Easy and Progressive Studies*, Op. 100, No. 15

*Practice and Performance Tips*
- The melody is in the left hand up to measure 19.
- Practice the left hand separately. Eventually the sixteenth notes in measures 3–4 and 11–12 should sound graceful and soft.
- The right-hand chords up to measure 19 need to be played very evenly and crisply.
- There is an indication at the beginning of *misterioso*, which is an apt description of the sly and light, mischievous character of the music.
- The character changes for the middle section, beginning at measure 31, with a smooth right-hand melody and gentle accompaniment chords in the left hand.
- Burgmüller has given us a narrative through the dynamic contrasts, painting a colorful story.

- In the coda at measure 87, practice hands separately until you can maintain tempo and evenness.

## PAUL CRESTON
(1906–1985, American)

Paul Creston was born into a poor Italian immigrant family in New York. As a child he took piano and organ lessons but was self-taught in theory and composition. In 1938 Creston was awarded a Guggenheim Fellowship, and in 1941 the New York Music Critics' Circle Award. He served as the director of A.S.C.A.P. from 1960–1968, and was composer-in-residence and professor of music at Central Washington State College from 1968–1975. His works, which include orchestral, vocal, piano, and chamber music repertoire, often feature shifting rhythmic patterns. He wrote a number of solos for instruments customarily left out of the limelight, such as the marimba, accordion, or saxophone. Creston was an important composition teacher (John Corigliano studied with him), and also wrote the books *Principles of Rhythm and Rational Metric Notation*.

### Toy Dance from *Five Little Dances*, Op. 24, No. 3
(composed 1940)

*Practice and Performance Tips*
- Begin practice hands separately.
- Keeping the left-hand accompaniment steady, even, soft and constantly *staccato* will take some practice.
- Most important is the composer's indication "very crisp."
- Except for some occasional slurred notes in the right hand, the entire piece is played *staccato*.
- The sharp contrast to $f$ only happens twice: measures 31–32 and 35–36.
- "Stiffly" refers to rhythm and articulation, and does not mean that your hand should be stiff in playing!
- Use no sustaining pedal at all.

## ALBERT ELLMENREICH
(1816–1905, German)

During his lifetime Ellmenreich was known mostly as an actor, playwright and theatre director, working in many cities in Germany. After many years of the touring life he retired from the stage in 1884. Ellmenreich was also an occasional composer of short character piano pieces, of which the "Spinning

Song" has become an indispensable standard in international student repertoire.

**Spinning Song**
**from *Musikalische Genrebilder*, Op. 14, No. 5**
*Musikalische Genrebilder* from 1863 is translated as *Musical Genre Pieces*. The title refers to someone working at a spinning wheel, spinning fibers into thread. Spinning songs were a common musical convention of the early Romantic period. The worker seems cheerfully content with the activity and enjoying her accomplishment, fluent and graceful at her task.

*Practice and Performance Tips*
- Practice hands separately.
- It's very important to accurately play the composer's detailed articulation.
- The job of the left hand in measures 1–26 and 52–79 is a steady, even, *staccato* accompaniment to the right hand.
- The composer did not mark the repeated notes of the right-hand accompaniment *staccato* in measures 27–42. Play these evenly and gently.
- *Allegretto* is an indication of a gentle speed, not racing ahead.

## MORTON GOULD
(1913–1996, American)

Morton Gould was born in Queens to an Australian father and a Russian mother. He composed his first work, a waltz for piano, when he was six. At eight he entered the Institute of Musical Art, which would later become The Juilliard School. His first work was published by G. Schirmer in 1932 when he was eighteen. Gould was a distinctly American presence, writing in both popular and contemporary classical styles and proving himself adept at conquering the rising mediums of radio and cinema. In the 1930s he played piano in vaudeville acts and at cinemas and dance studies. For radio he composed commercial jingles and radio symphonettes, and he also worked as a conductor, arranger, and composer for WOR New York's weekly "Music for Today" program. In 1933, Stokowski premiered his *Chorale and Fugue in Jazz* with the Philadelphia Orchestra. Gould wrote in various styles and blurred the lines between classical and popular music. Besides concert works he also wrote for Broadway. His works were performed by the New York Philharmonic, the Cleveland Orchestra, and other leading orchestras. In 1994 he was awarded a Kennedy Center Honor for his contributions to American culture, and in 1995 he

won the Pulitzer Prize for his final orchestral work, *Stringmusic*, which he wrote on commission for the National Symphony Orchestra as a farewell to Mstislav Rostropovich.

**Birthday Bells from *At the Piano*, Book 1**
*At the Piano* (Books 1 and 2) was written in 1964 for Gould's daughter Deborah as she studied piano.

*Practice and Performance Tips*
- The composer's words "loud and happy" apply to the sections marked $f$ and $ff$ only.
- Practice the right hand separately and slowly, especially noting the parallel fourths in measures 9–10, 15–22, and 27–28.
- Practice the left hand separately and slowly in measures 29–30.
- Then move to practicing hands together, but slowly, and without pedal.
- Increase the tempo in your practice as you master the music. But whatever tempo, keep it steady throughout.
- The composer has indicated several changes in dynamics. Take note!
- Gould wrote, "Use plenty of pedal!" We have made an editorial suggestion of pedaling.

## GEORGE FRIDERIC HANDEL
(1685–1759, German/British)

Handel was one of the defining composers of the Baroque period. After a brief time in Italy as a young man, he spent nearly his entire adult career in London, where he became famous as a composer of opera and oratorio, including *Messiah*, now his most recognizable music. Handel also wrote numerous concertos, suites, overtures, cantatas, trio sonatas, and solo keyboard works. Though he taught some students early in his career and occasionally instructed members of the London aristocracy, Handel was not known for his teaching abilities. His keyboard works were likely not written for any of his students, but to fulfill commissions or generate income from publication. Handel composed various keyboard works until 1720, then he became master of the orchestra for the Royal Academy of Music, an organization dedicated to performing new operas. After Italian opera fell out of fashion in London, Handel turned his compositional efforts to oratorio.

**Impertinence (Bourrée), HWV 494**
A bourrée is a lively dance movement, French in origin, from the Baroque, always in 2/2 or 4/4 meter, in binary form (meaning in two sections), and

beginning with a quarter-note upbeat. The bourrée became an optional part of the standard Baroque suite. Though it fell out of favor after the Baroque period among composers, the original folk dance is still found in the Auvergne region of France.

*Practice and Performance Tips*
- As with any fast music, begin practice slowly. In this piece, practice hands separately first.
- We have made stylistic suggestion of articulations (since these were not provided by the composer). Learning these articulations from the beginning of practice will help you achieve Baroque style.
- Carefully note the difference between the *staccato* notes and the slurred notes.
- After practicing each hand separately, move to practicing hands together, slowly.
- Gradually increase tempo as you master the music, always keeping a steady beat.
- The trills in measures 7 and 19 should begin on the note above. Handel's tempo *Vivace* is open for interpretation.
- There is wit in Handel's title of "Impertinence," indicating an irreverent rebel.

## FRANZ JOSEPH HAYDN
(1732–1809, Austrian)

One of the major composers of the eighteenth century, Haydn defined the sound of the Classical style. He was employed by the Esterházy court for the majority of his career, serving two Princes from the Hungarian ruling family in Vienna as well as in Hungary. Later in his life, Haydn spent time in London composing for the German violinist and musical impresario Johann Peter Salomon (1745–1815). Haydn lived his last years in Vienna. He wrote in nearly every genre of his day including operas, symphonies, and chamber music. Though his keyboard music is not as well-known as his orchestral works, he wrote over 50 piano sonatas and a large assortment of other keyboard pieces. The nickname "Papa Haydn" refers to Haydn being the compositional father of the modern symphony.

### Country Dance in C Major
Even master composers such as the great Haydn wrote teaching pieces like this simple country dance, which has a folk flavor about it. This dance, likely composed in 1795, in three is certainly not a waltz, but something more deliberate on each beat, such as a ländler. Haydn gave us no markings about articulation in this piece. We have editorially suggested articulation in period style.

*Practice and Performance Tips*
- Typical of this period for short pieces, the composer added few dynamics and articulations. We have made editorial suggestions to capture the style.
- Notice the notes marked slurred, contrasted with the notes marked *staccato*.
- Haydn is known for surprises as a composer, and the sudden triplet figure in measure 10 is certainly a surprise.
- Practice measures 10–11 hands separately.
- Make sure to keep a steady tempo through the triplets in measures 10–11. Don't slow down for this spot.
- Probably best to use no sustaining pedal.

## STEPHEN HELLER
(1813–1888, Hungarian/French)

Heller begged his parents for piano lessons as a child. At the age of seven he was already writing music for a small band put together by his father. The boy was sent to Vienna to study with Carl Czerny, but quickly found the lessons too expensive and instead studied with Anton Halm, who introduced Heller to Beethoven and Schubert. At age 13 Heller was giving concerts in Vienna as a pianist and two years later began touring Europe. His travels brought him in contact with Chopin, Liszt, Paganini, and most importantly Robert Schumann, with whom he developed a life-long friendship. Heller even contributed to Schumann's journal *Neue Zeitschrift* under the pseudonym Jeanquirit. After two years of touring, the rigorous schedule became too much for the boy and Heller settled first in Ausburg, and then in Paris to teach and compose. He wrote several hundred piano pieces, of which the short character pieces from opuses 45, 46, and 47 are frequently performed today.

### Allegretto ("Scampering")
### from *25 Etudes*, Op. 47, No. 1
The original French title of the set from 1849 is *25 Etudes pour former au sentiment du rhythme et á l'expression* (*25 Etudes to form a sense of rhythm and expression*). The titles, such as "Scampering," were added in later editions; the pieces are without title in the original edition.

*Practice and Performance Tips*
- Because of the nature of the music, best to begin practice slowly and hands together measures 1–14, rather than separately.

- Practice hands separately in measures 15–19 and 28–34.
- Aim for smoothness and evenness in the sound as the music is passed back and forth from hand to hand.
- The scampering here is of the most graceful variety. Make sure your *Allegretto* isn't too fast.
- The composer breaks the pattern in measure 15; the texture changes to sixteenths in the right hand and the rhythmic motion slows in measure 20.
- This break allows the return of the opening material to sound fresh, but it is a deceptive recapitulation. Heller only gives us the first three measures of the idea before abandoning it and moving into a free variation to the end.
- Heller has completely composed every detail of articulation and dynamic for the pianist. Observe them carefully!

## ALAN HOVHANESS
(1911–2000, American)

Alan Hovhaness was born in Somerville, Massachusetts, and studied at the New England Conservatory with Frederick Converse. He became interested in the music of India, to which he was exposed by musicians in the Boston area, and later looked to his Armenian heritage as well as music from Japan and Korea for inspiration. A prolific composer, Hovhaness' over five hundred works include all the major genres of western art music. He wrote six ballets as well as other stage works, sixty-six symphonies, works for chorus and voice, plus numerous chamber and piano pieces. One of his most well-known works is his Symphony No. 2 *Mysterious Mountain*, premiered by Leopold Stokowski and the Philadelphia Orchestra in 1955. His career went through a number of stages, incorporating aspects from the Renaissance and the Romantic era in addition to traditions outside Western classical music. Despite these shifts in style, he consistently sought to portray a connection between music, spirituality, and nature. Mountains particularly moved him, and he chose to live much of his life in Switzerland and the Pacific Northwest due to the proximity of these regions to the landscape that served as his muse.

### Moon Dance from *Mountain Idylls,* Op. 119, No. 2
This set composed in 1949 was subtitled "Three Easy Pieces for Piano." Published as set in 1955, the three pieces were written at various times. An idyll is a poem describing a pastoral, simple scene.

Hovhaness was particularly fond of mountains. "Moon Dance" is the easiest of the three pieces in the set.

*Practice and Performance Tips*
- Practice slowly, hands separately.
- Practice the right-hand melody, finding the phrasing and singing tone.
- Practice the left hand, creating the quiet and smooth movement of the broken triads.
- The piece asks for soft but sparkling tone. Imagine the gentle glistening of moonlight.
- Practice the pedaling Hovhaness has composed while playing the left hand alone.
- As you master the piece, move on to the *Allegro* tempo, keeping a steady beat throughout.

## DMITRI KABALEVSKY
(1904–1987, Russian)

Kabalevsky was an important Russian composer of the Soviet era who wrote music in many genres, including four symphonies, a handful of operas, theatre and film scores, patriotic music, choral music, vocal music, and numerous piano works. He embraced the Soviet notion of socialist realism in art, a fact that was politically advantageous to his career in the USSR. While studying piano and composition at the Moscow Conservatory, he taught piano lessons at a music college and it was for these students that he began writing works for young players. In 1932 he started teaching at the Moscow Conservatory, earning the title of professor in 1939. He eventually went on to develop programs for the concert hall, radio, and television aimed at teaching children about classical music. In the last decades of his life, Kabalevsky focused on developing music curricula for schools, retiring from the Moscow Conservatory to teach in public schools where he could test his theories and the effectiveness of his syllabi. This he considered his true life's work, and his pedagogical principles revolutionized music education in Russia. A collection of his writings on music education was published in English in 1988 as *Music and Education: A Composer Writes About Musical Education.*

### Selections from *30 Pieces for Children,* Op. 27
Kabalevsky often quoted Maxim Gorki, saying that books for children should be "the same as for adults, only better." Kabalevsky believed strongly in writing music for students that was not dumbed-down, but rather, complete, imaginative compositions unto themselves. The set was composed in 1937–38. Kabalevsky did a slight

revision of opus 27 in 1985, which was intended to be an authoritative edition. (This is our source for the pieces in this collection.)

### Toccatina (No. 12)

*Practice and Performance Tips*

- A toccata is a piece that shows brilliant playing. A toccatina is a miniature toccata.
- The left-hand melody should be predominant, marked *cantando* (singing), and played smoothly.
- The right-hand *staccato* chords are accompaniment to the left-hand melody.
- Practice the right hand separately, playing the chords crisply.
- Begin practice slowly, learning the phrasing, articulation and dynamics as you learn the notes and rhythms.
- Divide the piece into sections for practice. For instance, section 1: measures 1–18; section 2: measures 19–34; section 3: measures 35–49.
- Only increase the speed when you have mastered all the details.
- Do not play this music (marked *allegretto*) too quickly.
- Use no pedal throughout. Pedaling would blur the *staccato* chords in the right hand.

### Sonatina (No. 18)

*Practice and Performance Tips*

- Except for measure 41, the left hand is an accompaniment throughout to the right-hand melody.
- Begin practice hands separately at a slow tempo.
- Learn the phrasing as composed as you learn the right-hand melody.
- Even though the opening motive is rhythmic and rigorous, note that Kabalevsky has written a phrase over it.
- The *staccato* chords in the left hand should be played crisply.
- Divide the piece into sections for practice. For instance, section 1: measures 1–12; section 2: measures 13–24; section 3: measures 25–32; section 4: measures 33–43.
- Note the sudden shifts to *p* in measures 13 and 33.
- The only spots requiring pedal are as marked, measure 7 and measure 31, with the rolled chord in the left hand.
- Other than as marked, use no pedal.

**Almost a Waltz from 35 *Easy Pieces,* Op. 89, No. 33**
Kabalevsky's last large set of piano pieces for students was composed in 1972–74 when the composer was in his late sixties, after a lifetime of experiences with young musicians, and after he had attained a revered position as the cultural leader of music education in the USSR. These were also his last compositions for piano. After 1974 Kabalevsky only wrote a few more compositions, which were songs or small choral pieces.

*Practice and Performance Tips*

- In the meter changes the composer has indicated how the measure divides.
- 7/4 measures (most of the piece) are a combination of 4 beats + 3 beats, indicated by the dotted bar line.
- 6/4 measures are a combination of 3 beats + 3 beats, indicated by the dotted bar line.
- Because the quarter note stays the same throughout, these meters are not difficult to comprehend.
- Keep the quarter-note beat steady throughout, except in the section marked *poco rit*.
- *Cantando* means singing, applied to the right-hand melody, which is to be played gracefully and smoothly.
- Divide the piece into sections for practice. For instance: section 1: measures 1–17; section 2: measures 18–25; section 3: measures 24–38.
- It is very important to release the pedal exactly as indicated.
- The right-hand melody should be slightly brought out above the accompaniment in the left hand.
- Do not take this piece too fast, which will destroy the tranquillo mood the composer requests.
- A performance of this piece should be graceful and elegant.

## ARAM KHACHATURIAN
(1903–1978, Soviet/Armenian)

Aram Khachaturian was a seminal figure in 20th-century Armenian and Soviet culture. Beloved in his homeland for bringing Armenia to prominence within the realm of Western art music, a major concert hall in Armenia's capital Yerevan bears his name, as well as a string quartet and an international competition for piano and composition. Born in Tbilisi, Georgia, of Armenian heritage, he grew up listening to Armenian folk songs but was also exposed to classical music early on through the Tbilisi's chapter of the Russian Music Society, the city's Italian Opera Theater, and visits by musicians such as Sergei Rachmaninoff. He moved to Moscow to study composition in

1921. Khachaturian's musical language combined Armenian folk influences with the Russian romantic tradition, embodying the official Soviet arts policy. He used traditional forms, such as theme and variations, sonata form, and Baroque suite forms, in creative ways, juxtaposing them with Armenian melodies and religious songs, folk dance rhythms, and a harmonic language that took inspiration from folk instruments such as the saz. He wrote symphonies, instrumental concertos, sonatas, ballets, and was the first Armenian composer to write film music. Khachaturian's most recognizable composition to the general public is "Sabre Dance" from the ballet *Gayane*. Starting in 1950, he also became active as an internationally touring conductor. He was awarded the Order of Lenin in 1939 and the Hero of Socialist Labor in 1973.

**You Can't Go Outside Today**
**from *Children's Album*, Book 1**
(composition begun 1926, completed 1947)
In a previous Schirmer edition, the editor gave the piece the title "Ivan Can't Go Out Today."

*Practice and Performance Tips*
- The composition expresses the restlessness and melancholy of a sick boy who has to stay in at home.
- Begin practice hands together at a slow, steady tempo.
- Pay careful attention to all of Khachaturian's phrases, accents, and dynamics.
- Learn the notes at a slow tempo before attempting Khachaturian's intricate pedaling.
- Divide the piece into sections for practice. For instance, section 1: measures 1–20; section 2: measures 21–36; section 3: measures 37–50; section 4: measures 51–62; section 5: measures 63–73; section 6: measures 74–86.
- Only increase the tempo in your practice when you have mastered all the details.
- Be sure to keep a steady tempo throughout, until the *ritardando* near the end.

**Bedtime Story**
**from *Children's Album*, Book 2**
(composed 1965)
*Practice and Performance Tips*
- Practice the right-hand waltz melody separately, finding the smooth *cantabile* (singing tone) the composer indicates.
- Divide the piece into sections for practice. For instance: section 1: measures 1–23; section 2: measures 23–35; section 3: measures 36–55.
- The composer's phrase markings are the key to finding the shape of this graceful, melancholy melody.
- The two chords in the left-hand waltz accompaniment should be played with slight separation.
- The texture of the music changes in the middle section, beginning in measure 23, with the heavy accents in the repeated notes of the right hand.
- The slurred *staccatos* in the left hand in measures 24, 26 and 28 should be shaped as a phrase, with slight separation.
- The smooth *legato* tone of the melody returns in measure 36.
- Khachaturian only indicates pedaling in the final measures. By implication, there is to be no pedal used elsewhere.

# WOLFGANG AMADEUS MOZART
(1756–1791, Austrian)

One of the most astonishing talents in the history of music, Mozart was first a child prodigy as a composer, keyboard player and violinist. He developed into one of the greatest composers who has ever lived, with a vast output in opera, symphonies, choral music, keyboard music, and chamber music, all accomplished before his death at the young age of 35. Mozart spent most of his adult life living and working in Vienna. He was at the end of the era when successful musicians and composers attained substantial royal court appointments. A major position of this sort eluded him, despite his enormous talent, and he constantly sought opportunities to compose and perform. His music embodies the eighteenth century "age of reason" in its refined qualities, but adds playfulness, earnestness, sophistication and a deep sense of melody and harmony. Mozart's piano sonatas, concertos, sets of variations, and many other pieces at all levels from quite easy to virtuosic have become standards in the literature. His first compositions as a boy, from age five, were for keyboard. The notes on the individual pieces below were adapted from material previously published in *Mozart: 15 Easy Piano Pieces* (Schirmer Performance Editions).

**Minuet in G Major, K. 1e/1f**
(composed 1761–62)
The trio originated in the Baroque period as a contrast to the minuet. It was often performed by three players (hence, the labeling of "trio").

*Practice and Performance Tips*
- Begin practice slowly and hands separately.
- Keep a very steady beat throughout all practice.

- This music asks for refined and even touch. Flaws in playing will be exposed.
- After you have mastered the music, practice it *p*, without slowing down.
- Graceful articulation in the appropriate style is shown in the editorial suggestions (in brackets).
- After playing the trio, in the return to the minuet, do not play the repeats.

### Allegro in B-flat Major, K. 3

This little piece is dated March 1762, almost entirely written in only two voices, with a third voice added only to reinforce the tonic chord in measures 4, 6, 24, and 26. There are many editorial suggestions regarding articulation, which will help find the appropriate style. Notice a suggested *decrescendo* and *ritardando* in measures 27 and 28 on the second time only, followed by a recommended *mf* a tempo.

*Practice and Performance Tips*
- Begin practice slowly and hands separately.
- Graceful articulation in the appropriate style is shown in the editorial suggestions (in brackets). If you learn this right away, as you learn the notes and fingering, rather than learning it later, it will make it easier to achieve the style.
- After playing the trio, in the return to the minuet, do not play the repeats.
- Mozart's music requires clarity and evenness.
- Make sure your *allegro* doesn't become too fast.
- Use no sustaining pedal.

# ROBERT MUCZYNSKI
(1929–2010, American)

Composer and pianist Robert Muczynski studied at DePaul University in his hometown of Chicago with Alexander Tcherepnin. A brilliant pianist, at twenty-nine he made his Carnegie Hall debut with a performance of his own compositions. In addition to solo piano works, Muczynski mainly wrote for small chamber ensembles and also composed several orchestral pieces. His flute and saxophone sonatas, as well as *Time Pieces* for clarinet and piano, have become part of the standard repertoire for those instruments. In 1981, his concerto for saxophone was nominated for the Pulitzer Prize. Muczynski was composer in residence on the faculty of the University of Arizona from 1965 until his retirement in 1988.

### Fable No. 3 from *Fables*, Op. 21, No. 3

This set composed in 1965 is subtitled "Nine Pieces for the Young," and was written for an eight-year-old piano student. About *Fables* the composer stated, "Few people realize how difficult it is to compose a piece that stays within the restrictions of that level. You have to restrain yourself when it comes to key choice, rhythmic complexity, and range. In *Fables* I tried to use strong patterns with the idea of liberating one hand by assigning it a repeating rhythmic or melodic figure." [1] Learn the articulation from the beginning, along with the notes and rhythms. The right-hand melody predominates throughout. It should be slightly brought out over the left-hand accompaniment. Notice that the composer has marked *senza pedale* (without pedal), and only indicates pedal on the last chord.

[1] From the preface to *Robert Muczynski: Collected Piano Pieces*, G. Schirmer, 1990.

*Practice and Performance Tips*
- Begin practice hands alone, at a slow tempo.
- Learn the articulation from the beginning, along with the notes and rhythms.
- The right-hand melody predominates throughout. It should be slightly brought out over the left-hand accompaniment.
- Move to practicing hands together, at a slow practice tempo.
- As you master the notes, rhythms, articulations and dynamics, increase your practice tempo, but always retain a steady beat.
- Notice that the composer has marked *senza pedale* (without pedal), and only indicates pedal on the last chord.

# CHRISTIAN PETZOLD
(1677–1733, German)

Only a little of the music by one of the greatest of Baroque organists survives. Were it not for the two popular minutes copied into the *Notebook for Anna Magdalena Bach*, Petzold might be completely forgotten today. Very little is known of his life apart from records of various organ concerts around Europe. He held a court position in Dresden, where he played and taught some of the major organists of the next generation.

### Minuet in G Major, BWV Appendix 114

J.S. Bach copied the following piece by Petzold, previously believed to have been composed by Bach, into the second volume (1725) of the *Notebook for Anna Magdalena Bach*. The notebooks were compiled for Bach's second wife.

*Practice and Performance Tips*
- We have no tempo from the composer for this famous minuet. We have given a range of metronomic values that would be appropriate to the style.
- Editorial suggestions regarding Baroque style has been suggested.
- Play the quarter notes not marked with a phrase slur slightly detached.
- The ornamentation in measures 3, 5 and 30 might be reserved for the repeat.
- Aim for graceful ease and evenness.
- Use no sustaining pedal.

## DOMENICO SCARLATTI
(1685–1757, Italian)

Domenico was one of two musical sons of composer Alessandro Scarlatti. Domenico was extraordinarily influential in the development of Italian solo keyboard music, composing nearly 600 sonatas for the instrument. He was taught by his father and other musicians in Naples until he secured the position of composer and organist for the royal chapel in Naples at the age of 15. He spent time in Venice and Rome serving as the Maestro di cappella at St. Peter's before moving to Lisbon, where he taught the Portuguese Princess. In 1728, he moved to Spain where he would spend the rest of his life, finally settling in Madrid, where he was the music master for the Princess and later Queen of Spain. A sonata in the Italian Baroque almost always meant a one-movement instrumental piece. Its musical form was not defined and could be many possibilities. The Italian Baroque style is distinctly different from the German Baroque style and the French Baroque style. Without going into complicated detail, the Italian Baroque style had more freedom than its German counterpart.

### Minuet from Sonata in C Major, L. 217 (K. 73b, P. 80)
Scarlatti's sonatas rarely include a minuet.

*Practice and Performance Tips*
- We have made editorial recommendations about slurring, *staccato* and dynamics that may help find Baroque style.
- Keep a very steady tempo.
- Notice the echo effect in measures 14–17.
- The trills should be added only in the second time through both sections.
- They should always begin on the note above and on the beat. This is also true of the final trill in the last measure.
- Tempo is open for interpretation, but it shouldn't be too fast.
- Use no sustaining pedal.

## ROBERT SCHUMANN
(1810–1856, German)

One of the principal composers of the Romantic era, Robert Schumann's relatively short creative career gave the world major repertoire in symphonies, art song, chamber music, and piano music. Besides being a composer, Schumann was an accomplished writer about music, especially as a critic, then editor of the influential *Neue Zeitschrift für Musik*. He was married to concert pianist Clara Wieck, who championed his works after his death, the result of a severe struggle with mental illness. Schumann was an early supporter of the young Johannes Brahms. Schumann made a specialty of short character pieces for piano, not entirely unrelated to his distinctive work as a major composer of art song.

### Selections from *Album for the Young (Album für die Jugend)*, Op. 68
This set of 43 pieces was composed in 1848 for Schumann's children. The first eighteen of the set are easier than those beginning with number 19, which are for a more mature pianist.

### Sicilienne (Sicilianish) (No. 11)
A siciliana or a sicilienne was traditionally a slow movement in 6/8 in the Baroque Era, rather like a slow gigue or jig. By the time of Schumann, the sicilienne had lost its Baroque characteristics, and composers sometimes used this label for pieces that tended to be in 6/8 and in the minor key.

*Practice and Performance Tips*
- Schumann doesn't exactly give a tempo, only a mood. Try a moderate tempo in the first section.
- The notes marked with *staccato* plus slur should be played with slight separation.
- As you practice hands alone, learn Schumann's detailed articulation and dynamics from the beginning, and apply it at any practice tempo. Schumann composed the articulation and dynamics as fully as he composed the notes and rhythms.
- The chords of the left hand in the fast section should be played with slight separation.
- Don't slow down in the last measure of the fast section. The music is meant to end abruptly.

- The fermata over the double bar lines at the end mean to rest a bit before the return to the beginning.

### Little Study (Kleine Studie) (No. 14)
*Practice and Performance Tips*
- This little study is based on arpeggiated chords. The left-hand notes always move upward; the right hand answers by moving downward.
- Schumann tells the pianist at the top of the piece to play "lightly and very evenly."
- Because there is constant interplay between the left and right hand, begin slow practice hands together rather than hands separately.
- To create phrasing, play slight arc from the beginning of the measure to the end of the measure.
- You may choose to slightly emphasize the first note in the right hand of each measure, because there is an implied melody that this first right-hand note constructs.
- It is important to understand the harmonic changes in each measure and to carefully make a pedal change on each new harmony.
- There is room for interpretation regarding tempo, since Schumann does not specifically tell us anything about the speed in his tempo marking.

## DMITRI SHOSTAKOVICH
(1906–1975, Russian)

A major mid-20th century composer, Shostakovich is famous for his epic symphonies, concertos, operas, string quartets, and other chamber works. Born in St. Petersburg, his entire career took place in Soviet-era Russia. His life teetered between receiving high official honors and living with an almost debilitating fear of arrest for works that did not adhere to the Soviet ideals of socialist realism. In 1934, his opera *Lady Macbeth of the Mtsensk District* met with great popular success, but was banned by Stalin for the next thirty years as modernist, surrealist, and obscene. The following year, Stalin began a campaign known as the Purges, executing or exiling to prison camps politicians, intellectuals, and artists. Shostakovich managed to avoid such a fate, and despite an atmosphere of anxiety and repression, was able to compose an astounding number of works with originality, humor, and emotional power. He succeeded in striking a balance between modernism and tradition that continues to make his music accessible to a broad audience. An excellent pianist, Shostakovich performed concertos by Mozart, Prokofiev, and Tchaikovsky early in his career, but after 1930 limited himself to performing his own works and some chamber music. He taught instrumentation and composition at the Leningrad Conservatory from 1937–1968, with brief breaks due to war and other political disruptions, and at the Moscow Conservatory in the 1940s. Since his death in 1975, Shostakovich has become one of the most-performed 20th century composers. Among a huge output of symphonies, operas and chamber music, Shostakovich wrote only a few pieces for piano students.

### The Mechanical Doll
**from *Children's Notebook for Piano*, Op. 69, No. 6**
*Children's Notebook for Piano* was written for his eight-year old daughter, Galina, for her studies on the instrument in 1944. "The Mechanical Doll" is occasionally known by other translated titles, such as "The Clockwork Doll."

*Practice and Performance Tips*
- Begin practice hands separately, and at a slow tempo.
- Divide the piece into sections for your practice. For instance: section 1 measures 1–16; section 2 measures 17–29; section 3: measures 30–45.
- Notice the imitation in measures 5-6, then again in measures 34–35, as the left hand follows the right hand with a similar phrase.
- Learn the articulation (slurs, *staccato*, accents) as you learn the notes and rhythms.
- When the left hand has the main melody in measures 30–33, it should sound just as strong and independent as when the right hand had the melody earlier.
- Move to practicing hands together, at a slow tempo, retaining the articulations you have learned when practicing hands alone.
- Keep a strict tempo, no matter what the speed.
- Be careful to observe the specific dynamics that are composed.
- Use no pedal at all. This music needs a crisp, playful touch throughout. Pedal would spoil the texture.

## PYOTR IL'YICH TCHAIKOVSKY
(1840–1893, Russian)

Tchaikovsky was the great Russian composer of the nineteenth century who achieved the most international success, and whose symphonies, ballets, operas, chamber music and piano music continue to be a central part of the repertoire. Of his piano works, *The Seasons*, Op. 37bis, *Album for the Young*, Op. 39 and his concerto are most familiar to present day pianists and teachers. *Album for the Young* was written in four days in May of 1878, with revisions later that year before publication in October. It was during this year that Tchaikovsky left his teaching post at the St. Petersburg Conservatory and began composing and conducting full time, a move made financially possible by the patronage of Nadezhda von Meck.

### The Doll's Funeral
**from *Album for the Young*, Op. 39, No. 8**
Much of *Album for the Young* (composed in 1878) is inspired by folksongs, capturing observations and experiences from childhood in 24 fanciful miniatures.

*Practice and Performance Tips*
- Probably begin practice at a louder level than *pp* when learning the piece.
- First practice without sustaining pedal. Then apply it, changing the pedal clearly with each change of harmony.
- Pay careful attention to dynamics. The music rises to its most dramatic and loudest point at the climax in measure 29.
- The procession that begins with the return of the opening music in measure 33. There is a funeral march quality to the music, as if the doll is being brought in procession to a backyard grave.

- The doll's funeral communicates both a sense of playful melodrama and earnest mourning.
- This is a funeral procession. Keep the tempo steady, as if it's accompanying a slow, steady walk.

### At Church
**from *Album for the Young*, Op. 39, No. 23**
*Practice and Performance Tips*
- Practice hands together and hands separately as necessary to learn the music.
- Practice first without sustaining pedal. Then add pedal on each change of harmony.
- The opening section, measures 1–12 and repeated in measures 13–24, sounds very much like a solemn Russian Orthodox hymn, a genre based more on modal than tonal harmony.
- Probably begin practice at a louder level than *pp* when learning the piece.
- Because the first statement of the hymn (measures 1–12) begins softly, and the second statement begins *mf* in measure 13, the composer perhaps creates the impression that the music increases in volume as one approaches the church.
- Because it is marked to be played *pp*, it's as if the listener is continuing past the church. The word *perdendosi* in measure 26 means dying away.

— Richard Walters, editor

*These pieces were previously published in the following*
*Schirmer Performance Editions volumes.*

Anonymous: Minuet in G Major, BWV Appendix 116
Anonymous: Musette in D Major, BWV Appendix 126
**from *J.S. Bach: First Lessons in Bach***
**edited by Christos Tsitsaros**

Bartók: Slovak Peasant Dance from *Ten Easy Pieces*
Creston: Toy Dance from *Five Little Dances*, Op. 24, No. 3
Gould: Birthday Bells from *At the Piano*, Book 1
Hovhaness: Moon Dance from *Mountain Idylls*, Op. 119, No. 2
Khachaturian: Bedtime Story from *Children's Album*, Book 2
Muczynski: Fable No. 3 from *Fables*, Op. 21, No. 3
**from *The 20th Century: Early Intermediate Level***
**edited by Richard Walters**

Sonatina in G Major, Kinsky-Halm Anh. 5, No. 1
**from *Beethoven: Selected Piano Works***
**edited by Matthew Edwards**

Sincerity (La Candeur)
Ballade
**from *Burgmüller: 25 Easy and Progressive Studies, Op. 100***
**edited by Margaret Otwell**

Ellmenreich: Spinning Song from *Musikalische Genrebilder*, Op. 14, No. 5
Heller: Allegretto ("Scampering") from *25 Etudes*, Op. 47, No. 1
**from *The Romantic Era: Early Intermediate Level***
**edited by Richard Walters**

Handel: Impertinence (Bourrée), HWV 494
D. Scarlatti: Minuet from Sonata in C Major, L. 217 (K. 73b, P. 80)
**from *The Baroque Era: Early Intermediate Level***
**edited by Richard Walters**

Haydn: Country Dance in C Major
**from *The Classical Era: Early Intermediate Level***
**edited by Richard Walters**

# Minuet in G Major

Christian Petzold
BWV Appendix 114

Fingerings, phrasing, and dynamics are editorial suggestions.

# Moon Dance
## from *Mountain Idylls*

Alan Hovhaness
Op. 119, No. 2

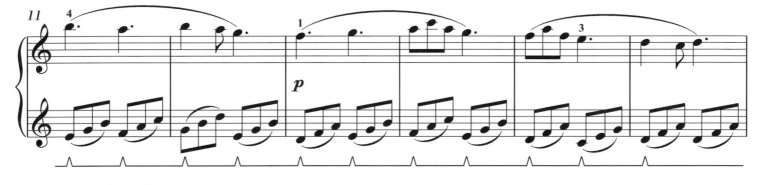

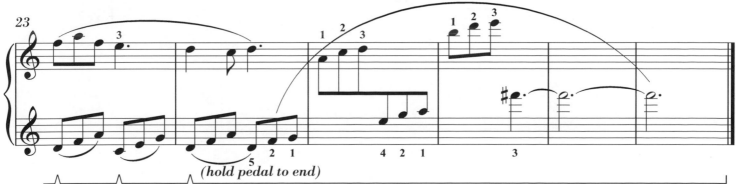

Fingerings are editorial suggestions.

# The Doll's Funeral
## from *Album for the Young*

Pyotr Il'yich Tchaikovsky
Op. 39, No. 8

Медленно [Slow] (♩ = 58–62)

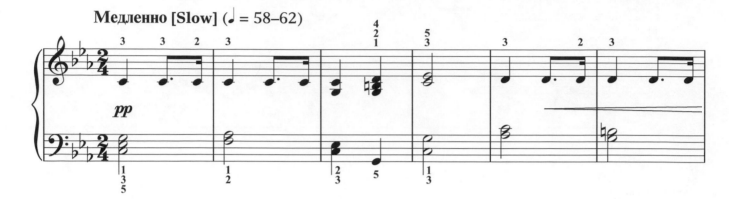

Fingerings are editorial suggestions.

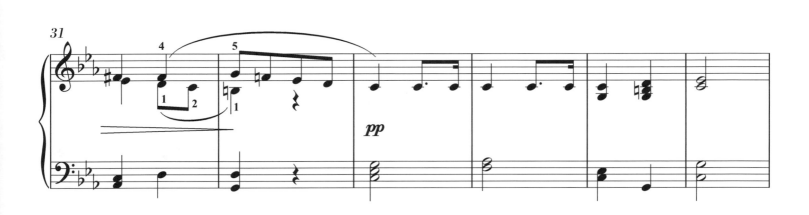

# At Church
## from *Album for the Young*

Pyotr Il'yich Tchaikovsky
Op. 39, No. 23

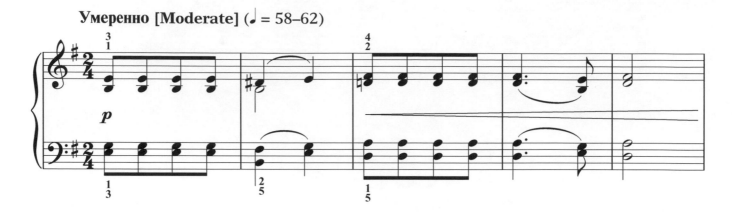

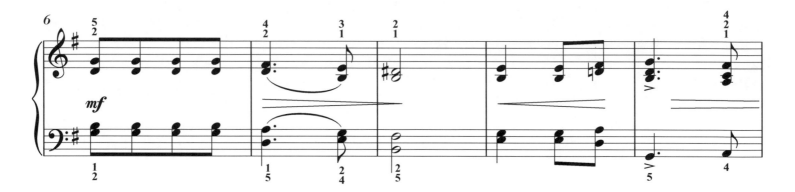

Fingerings are editorial suggestions.

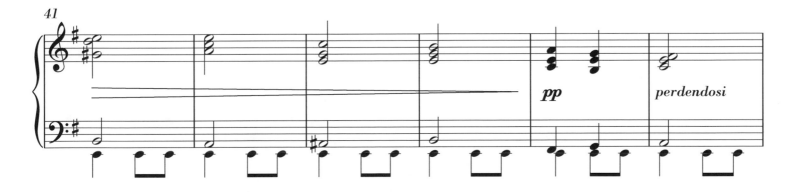

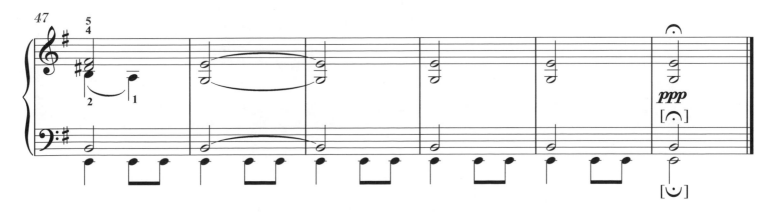

# Allegro in B-flat Major

Wolfgang Amadeus Mozart
K. 3

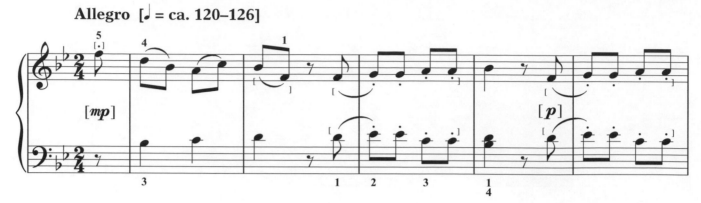

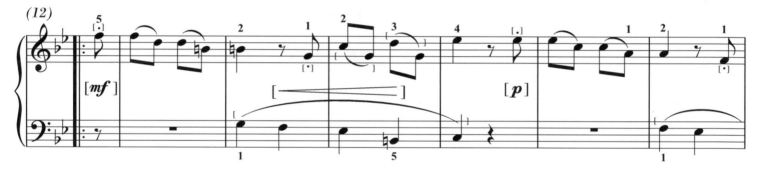

Fingerings are editorial suggestions.

# Country Dance in C Major

Franz Joseph Haydn

**Allegretto**

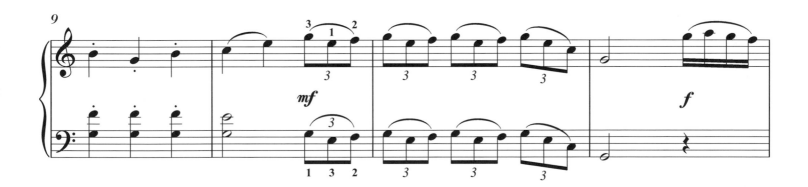

Fingerings, dynamics, and articulations are editorial suggestions.

# Sincerity
### (La Candeur)
## from *25 Easy and Progressive Studies*

Johann Friedrich Burgmüller
Op. 100, No. 1

**Allegro moderato ( ♩ = 152)**

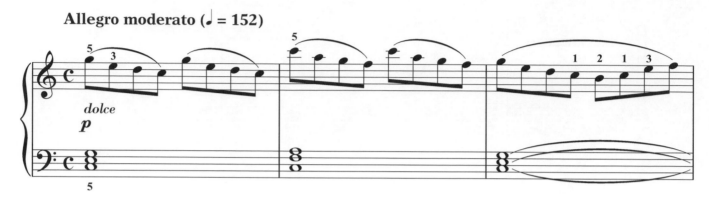

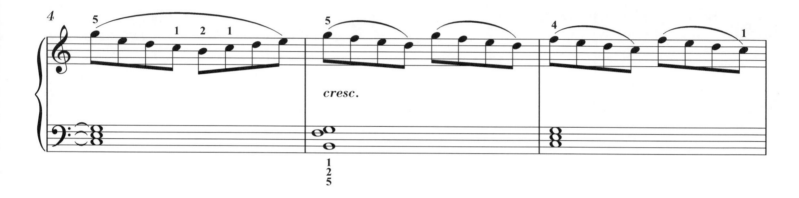

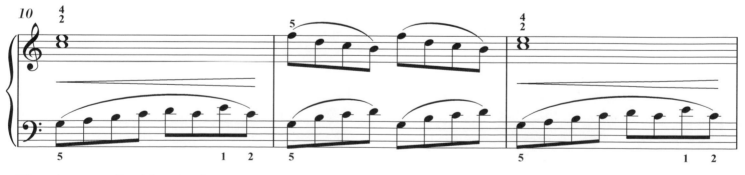

Fingerings are editorial suggestions.

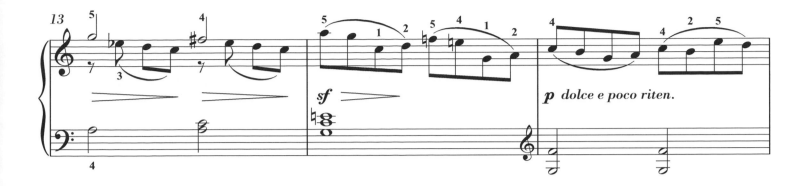

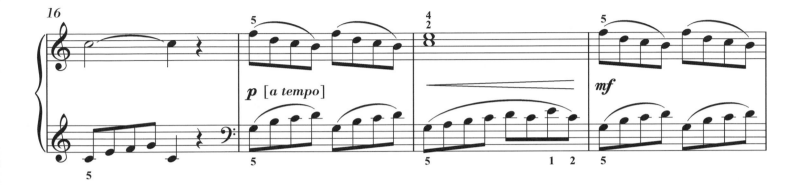

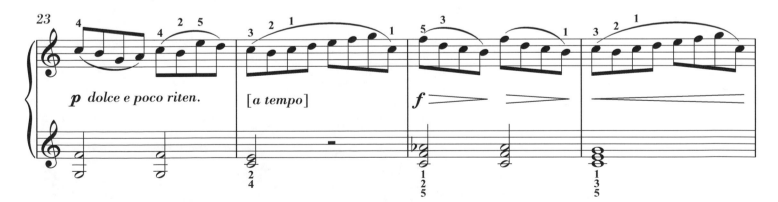

# Minuet in G Major

Wolfgang Amadeus Mozart
K. le/lf

[Andante ♩ = ca. 126]

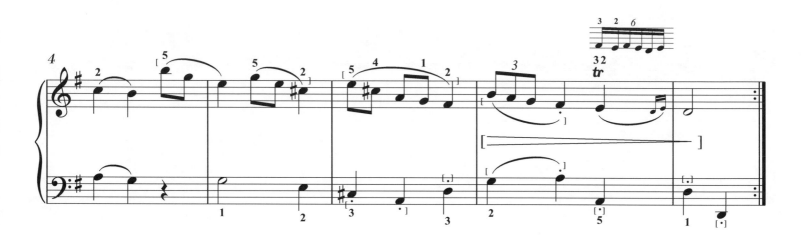

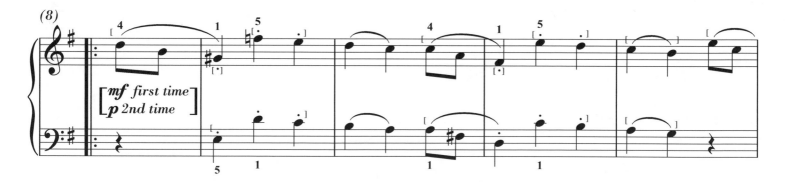

**Fine**
[*poco rit. last time*]

Eliminate repeats on the Da Capo.
Fingerings are editorial suggestions.

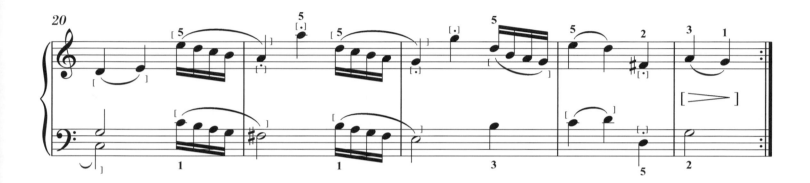

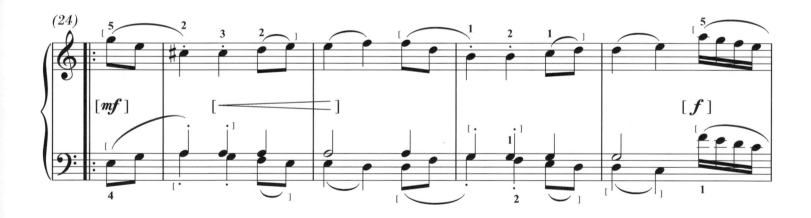

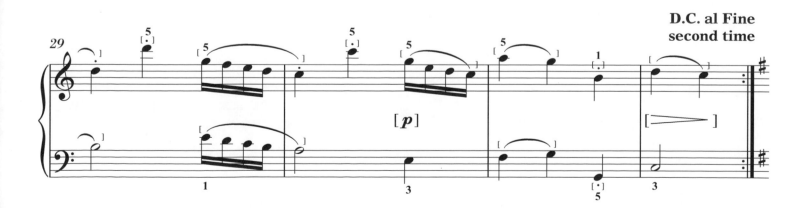

# Musette in D Major

Anonymous
BWV Appendix 126

**Moderato**

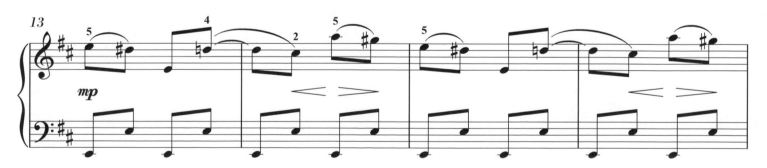

Fingerings, tempo, articulations and dynamics are editorial suggestions.

# Bedtime Story
## from *Children's Album*, Book 2

Aram Khachaturian

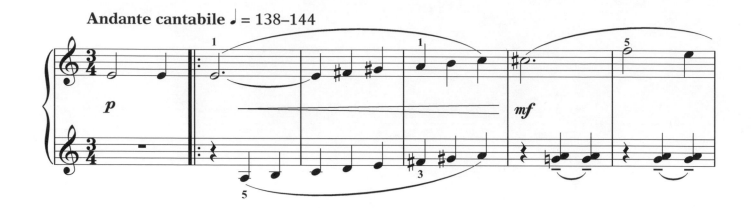

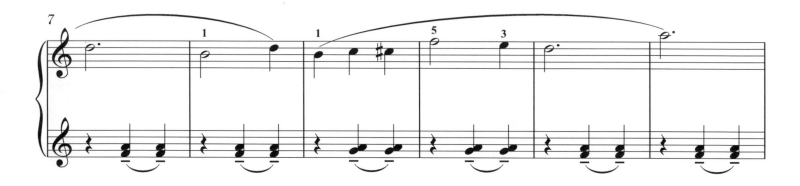

Fingerings are by the composer.

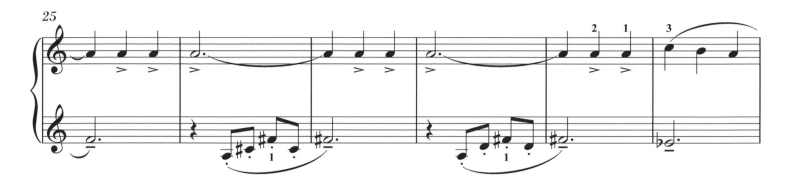

# Minuet in G Major

Anonymous
BWV Appendix 116

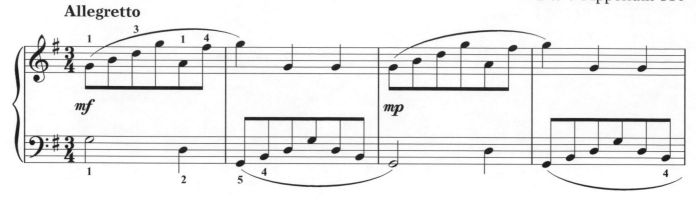

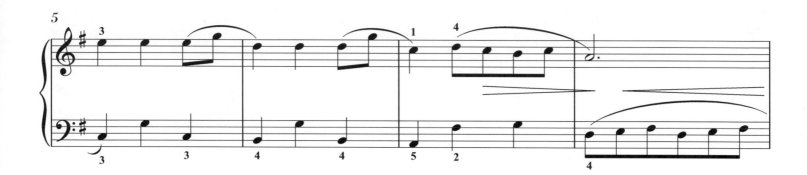

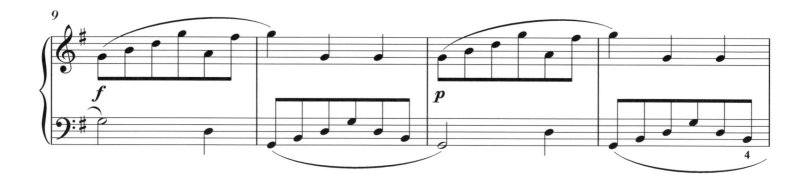

Fingerings, tempo, articulations, and dynamics are editorial suggestions.

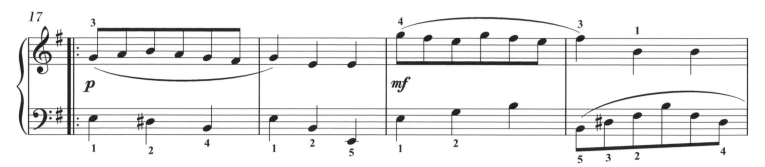

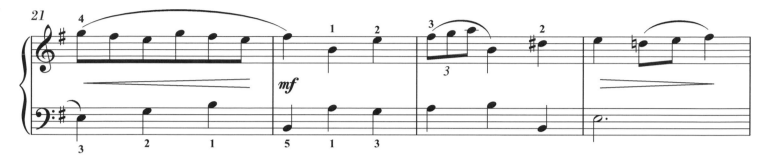

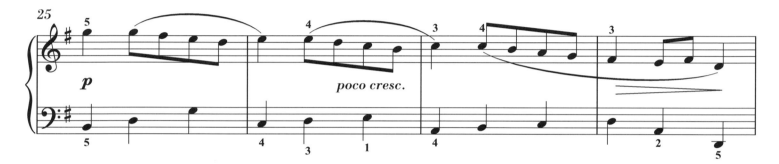

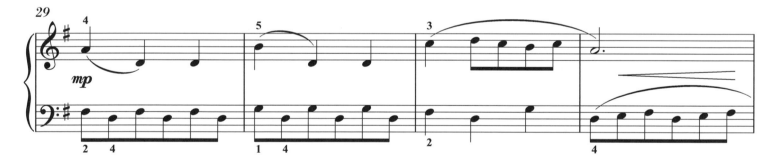

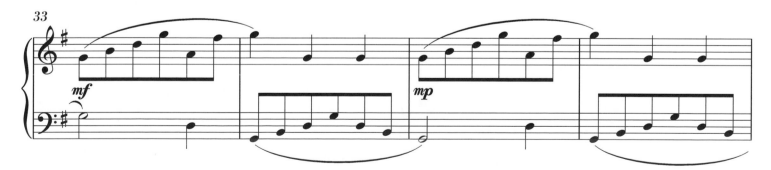

# Little Study
## (Kleine Studie)
### from *Album for the Young*

Robert Schumann
Op. 68, No. 14

**Leise und sehr egal zu spielen**
*Lightly and very evenly*

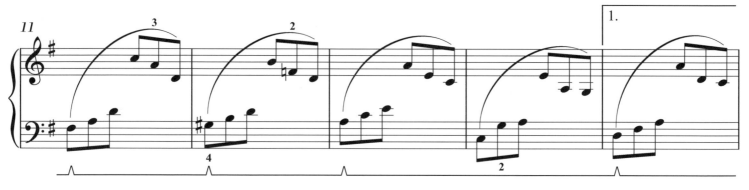

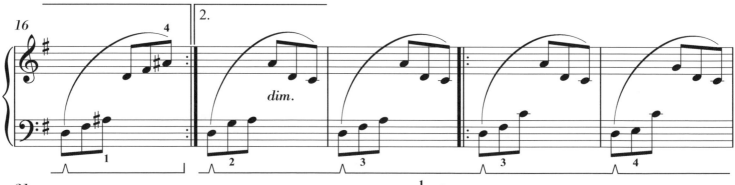

Fingerings are editorial suggestions.

23

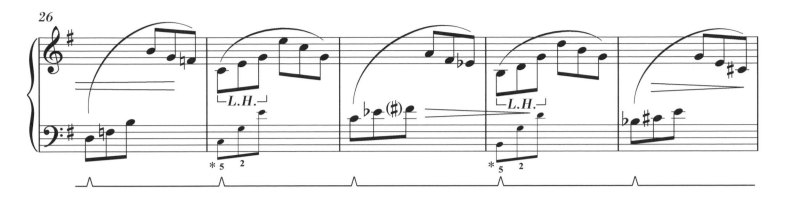

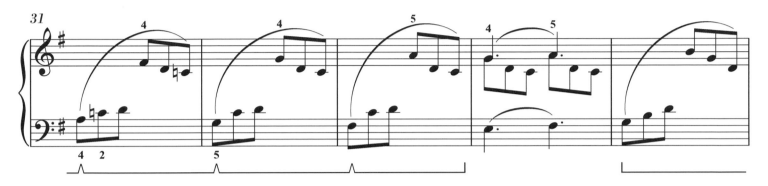

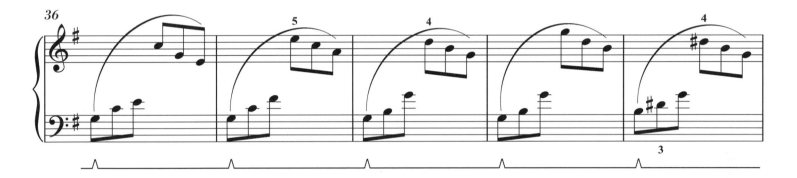

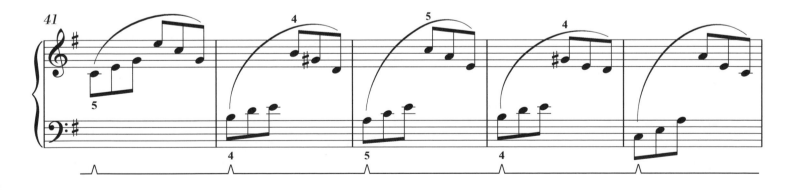

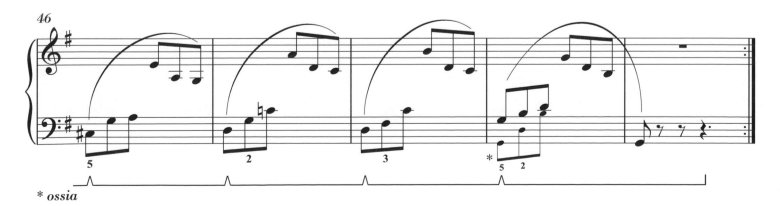

* ossia

# Birthday Bells
## from *At the Piano*, Book 1

Morton Gould

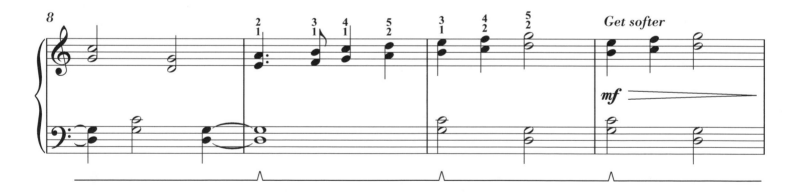

The pedaling is an editorial suggestion.
Fingerings are by the composer.

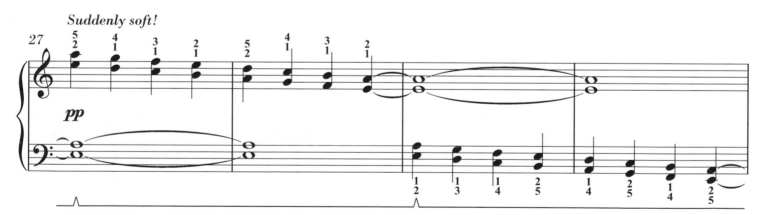

# Almost a Waltz

from *35 Easy Pieces*

Dmitri Kabalevsky
Op. 89, No. 33

Fingerings are by the composer.

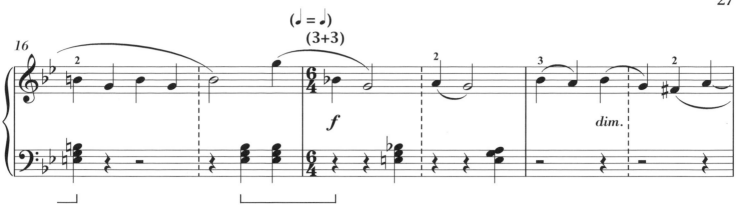

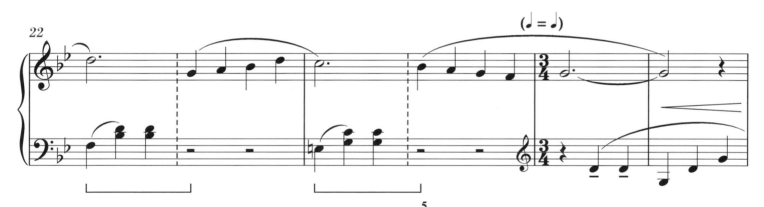

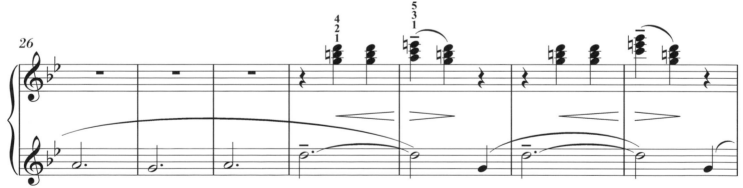

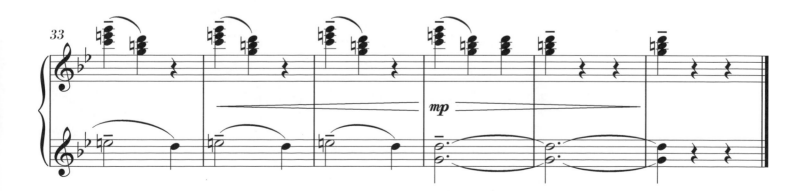

# Spinning Song

## from *Musikalische Genrebilder*

Albert Ellmenreich
Op. 14, No. 5

Fingerings are editorial suggestions.

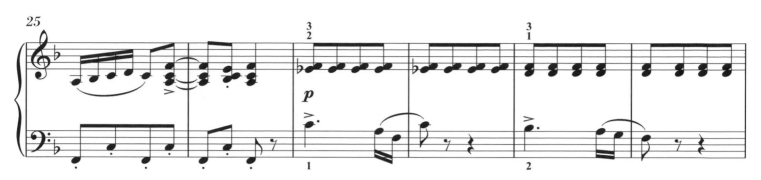

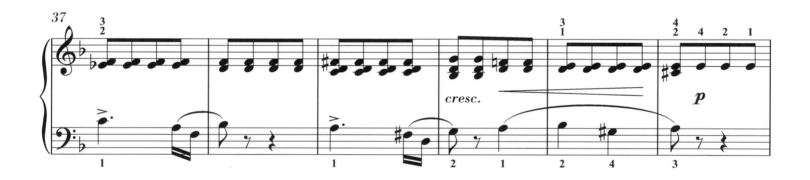

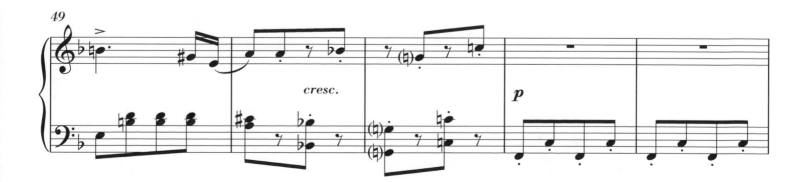

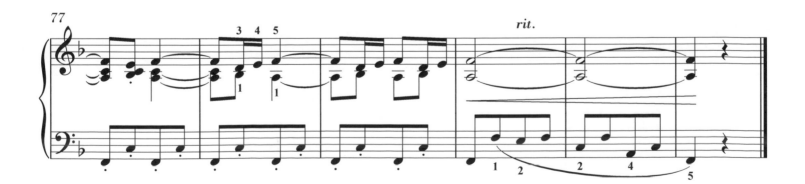

# You Can't Go Outside Today

from *Children's Album, Book 1*

Aram Khachaturian

**Allegro moderato**

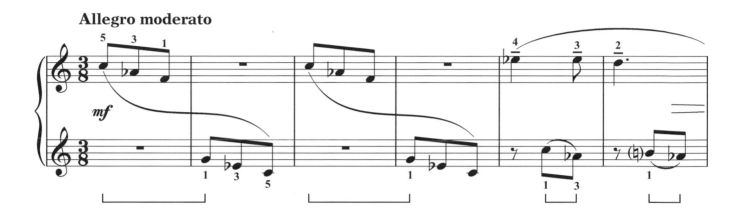

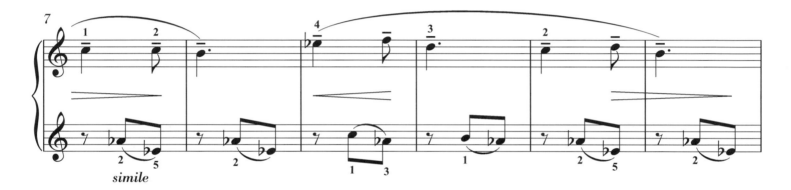

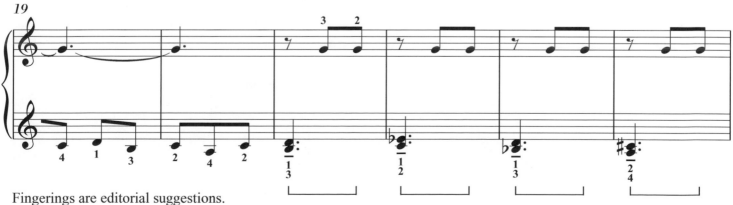

Fingerings are editorial suggestions.

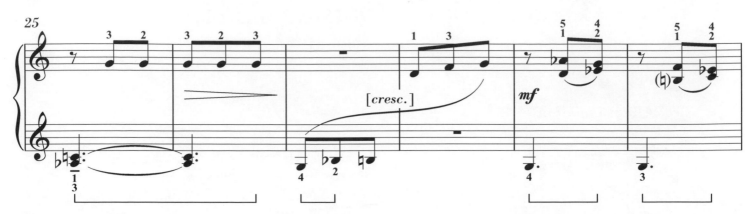

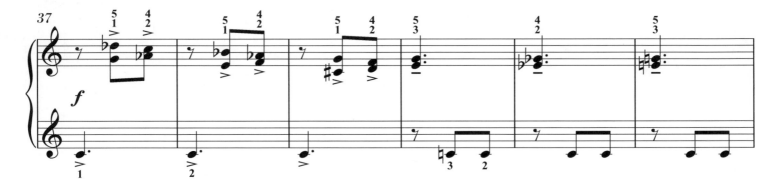

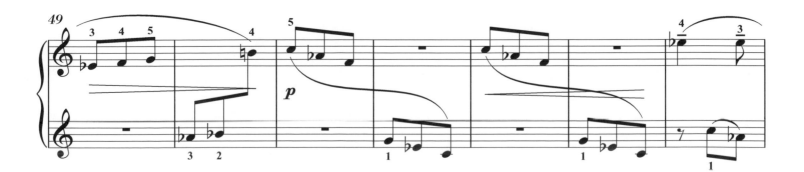

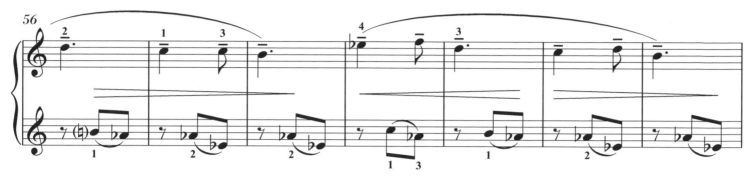

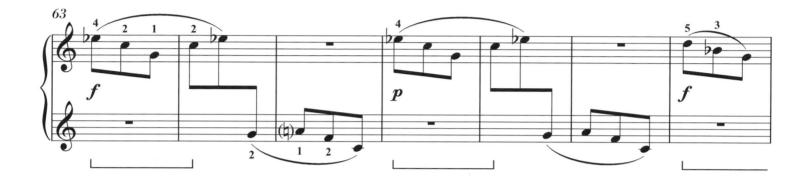

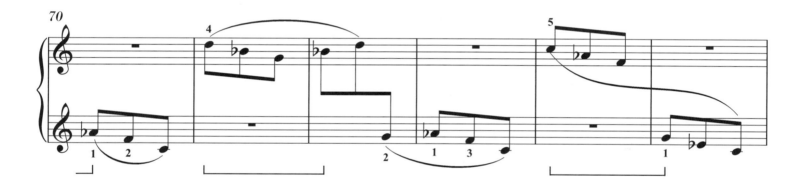

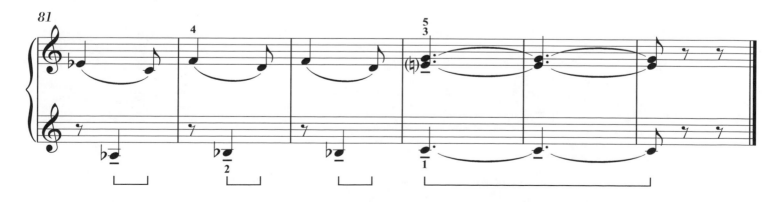

# Allegretto

## ("Scampering")

### from *25 Etudes*

Stephen Heller
Op. 47, No. 1

**Allegretto** (♩ = 80)

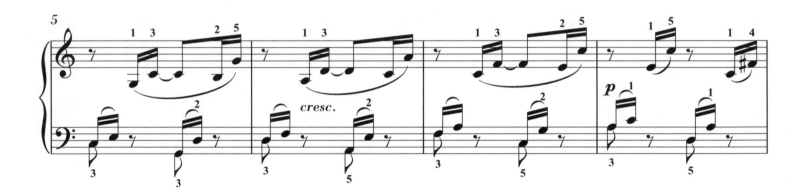

Fingerings are editorial suggestions.

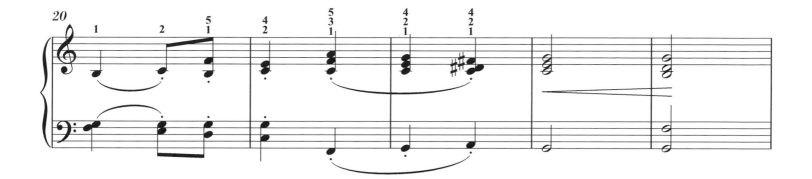

# Impertinence
## (Bourrée)

George Frideric Handel
HWV 494

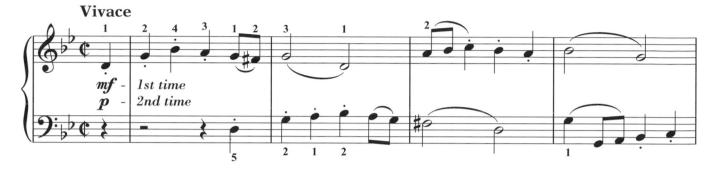

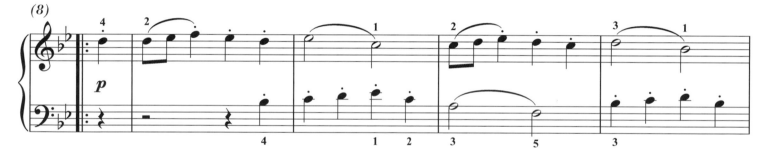

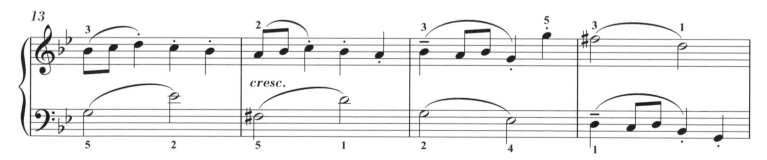

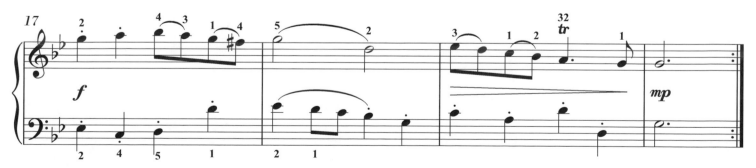

Fingerings, tempo, articulations, and dynamics are editorial suggestions.
Trills begin on the note above.

# Sicilienne
### (Sicilianisch)
from *Album for the Young*

Robert Schumann
Op. 68, No. 11

**Schalkhaft**
*Roguish*

Fingerings are editorial suggestions.

**Schluß**
*Fine*

**Schnell**
*Fast*

**Vom Anfang ohne Wiederholungen bis Schluß**
*From the beginning to Fine without repeat*

# Toccatina
## from *30 Pieces for Children*

Dmitri Kabalevsky
Op. 27, No. 12

**Allegretto [♩ = c. 110]**

*cantando*

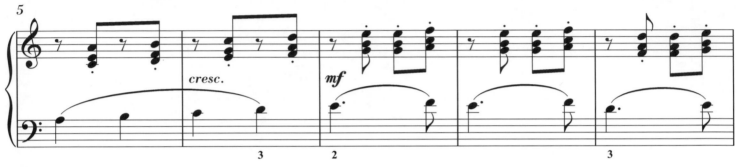

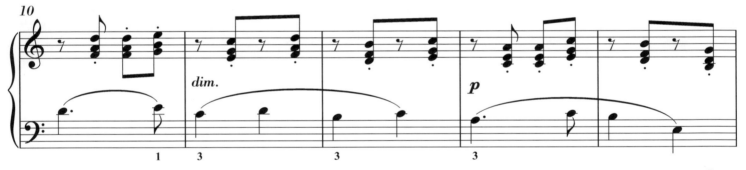

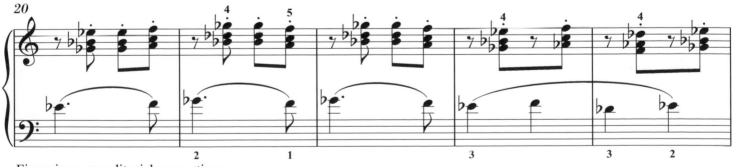

Fingerings are editorial suggestions.

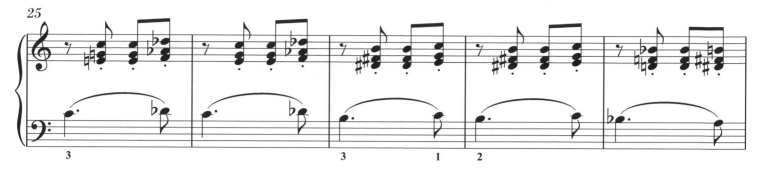

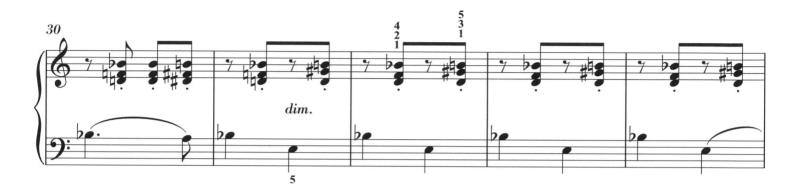

# Minuet
## from Sonata in C Major

Domenico Scarlatti
L. 217 (K. 73b, P. 80)

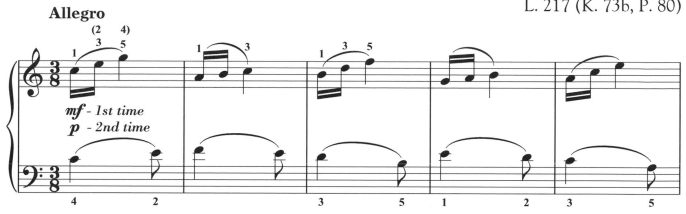

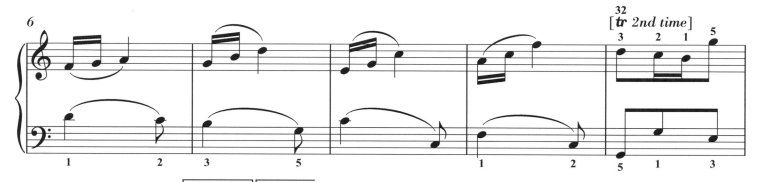

Fingerings, tempo, articulations, and dynamics are editorial suggestions.
Trills begin on the note above.

# Slovak Peasant Dance
### from *Ten Easy Pieces*

Béla Bartók

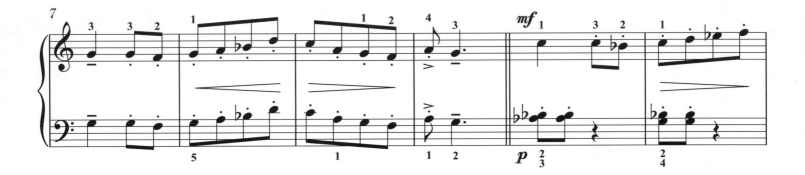

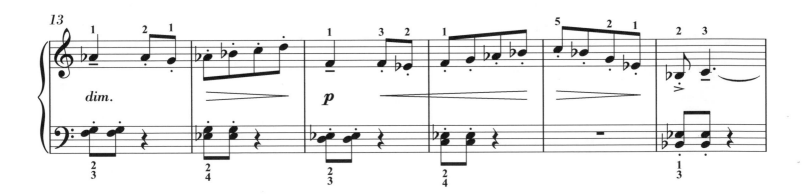

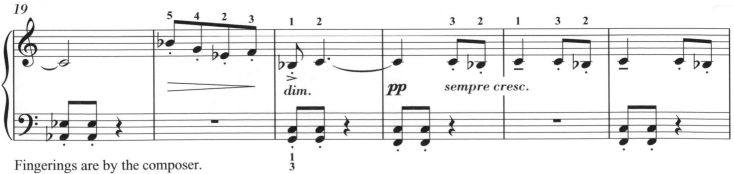

Fingerings are by the composer.

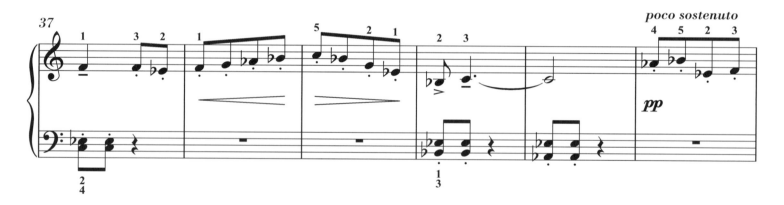

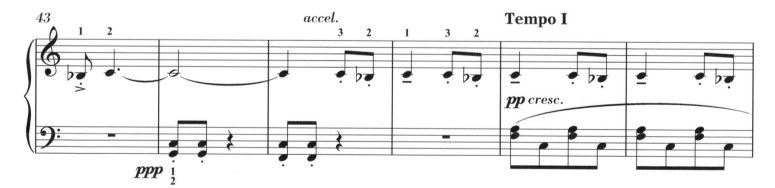

# Sonatina in G Major

## I

Ludwig van Beethoven
Kinsky-Halm Anh. 5, No. 1

**Moderato** [♩ = 126–132]

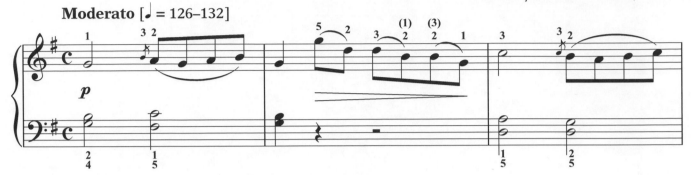

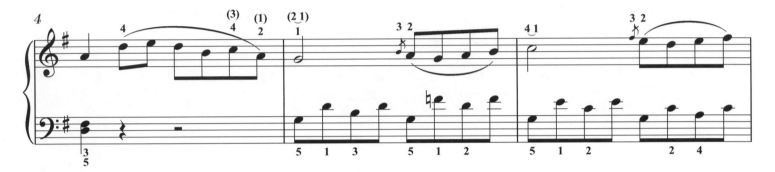

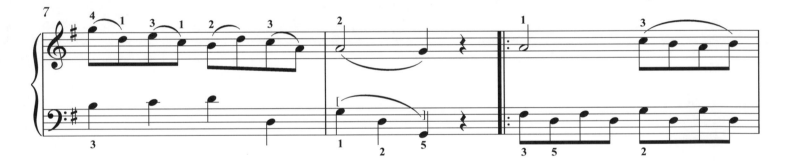

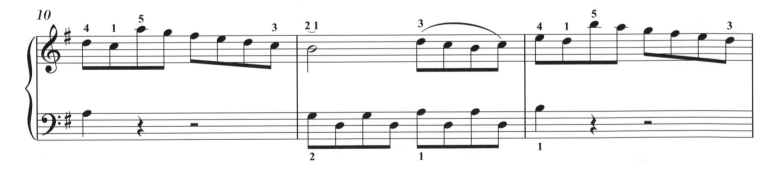

Fingerings are editorial suggestions.

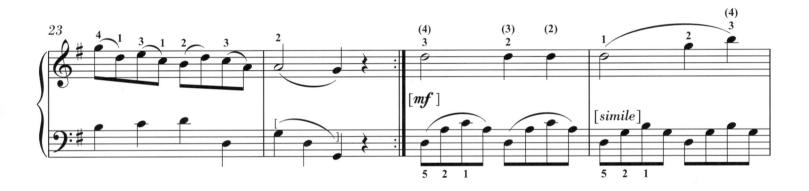

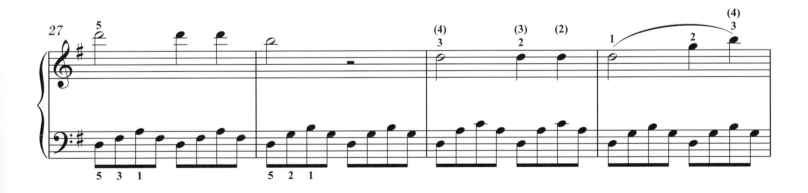

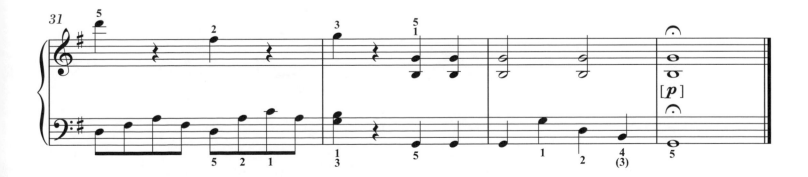

# II

Romanza [♩. = 63–69]

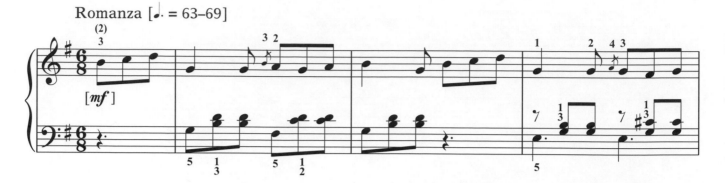

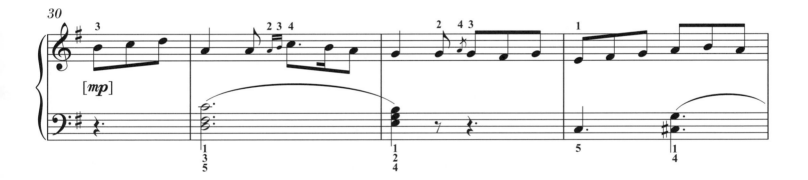

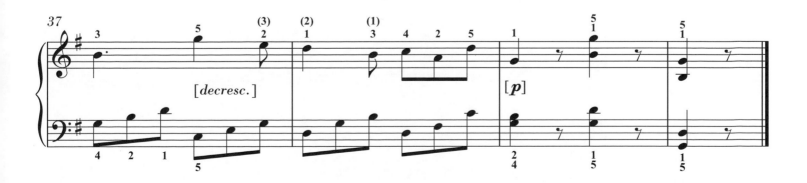

# Ballade

from *25 Easy and Progressive Studies*

Johann Friedrich Burgmüller
Op. 100, No. 15

**Allegro con brio** (♩. = 104)

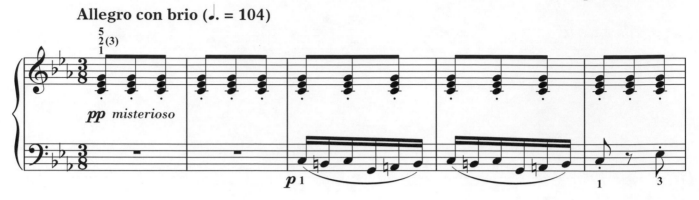

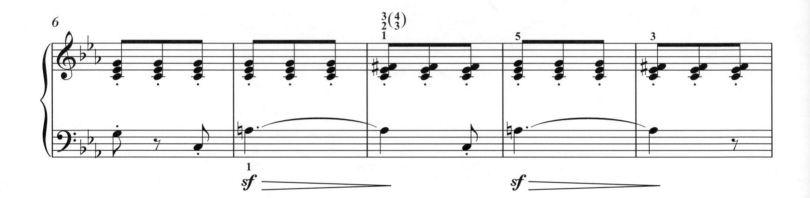

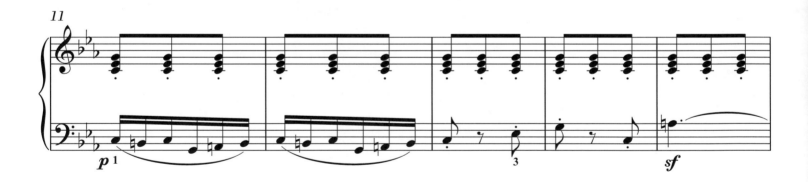

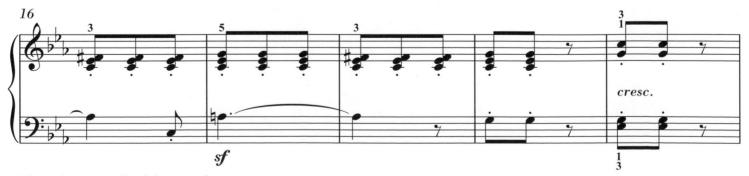

Fingerings are editorial suggestions.

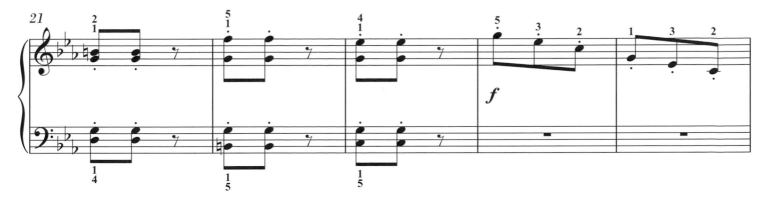

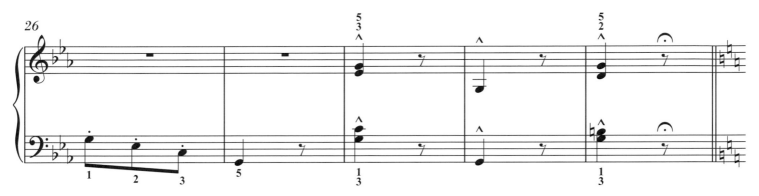

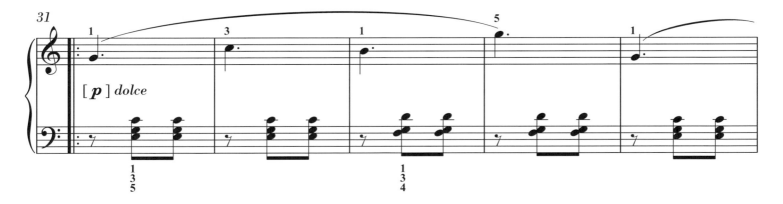

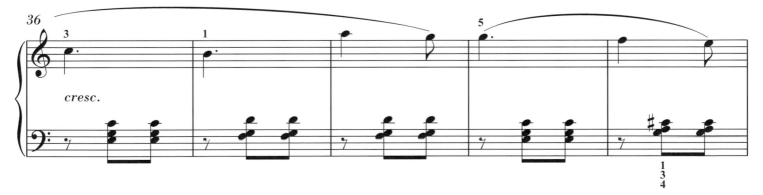

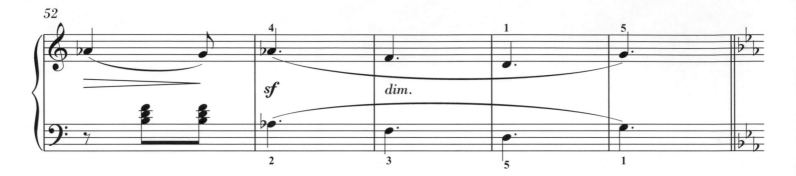

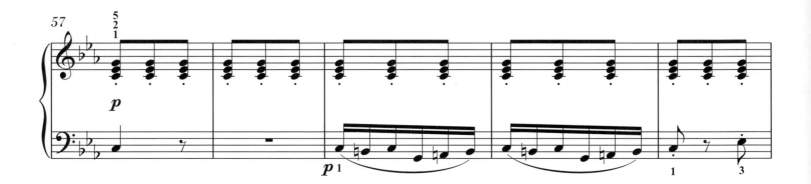

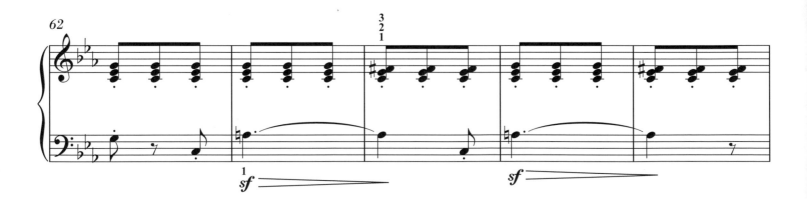

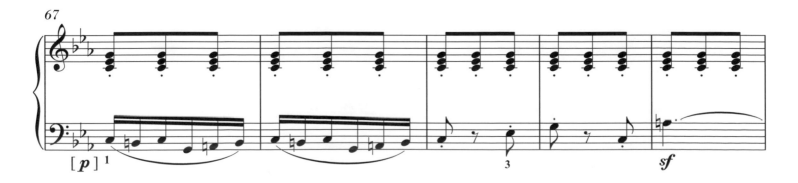

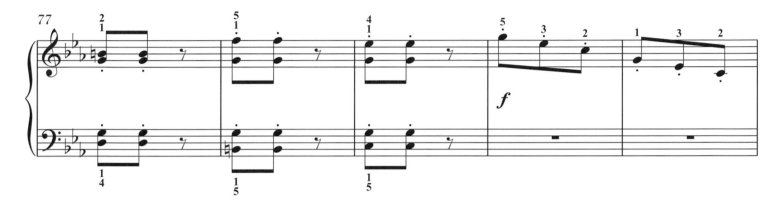

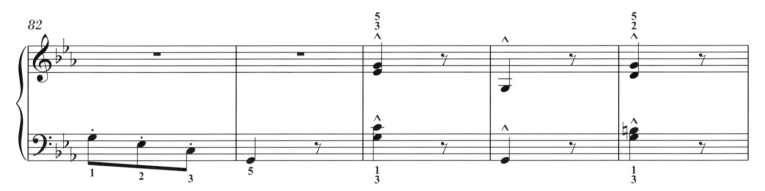

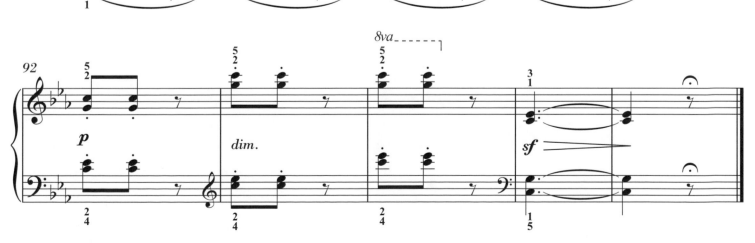

# Fable No. 3
## from *Fables*

Robert Muczynski
Op. 21, No. 3

**Allegro molto** ♩ = 144

*senza ped.*

Fingerings are by the composer.

# Toy Dance
## from *Five Little Dances*

Paul Creston
Op. 24, No. 3

**Stiffly** ♩ = 126

Fingerings are editorial suggestions.

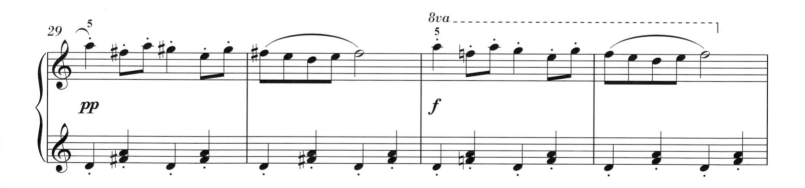

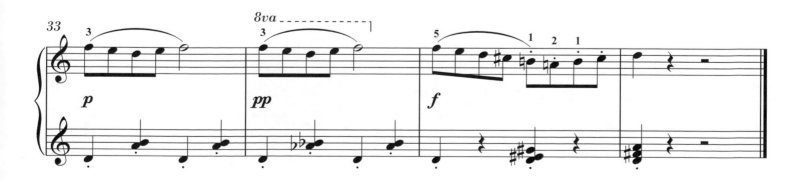

# The Mechanical Doll
## from *Children's Notebook for Piano*

Dmitri Shostakovich
Op. 69, No. 6

**Allegretto** [♩ = c. 88–92]

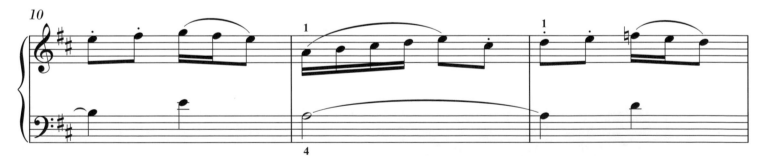

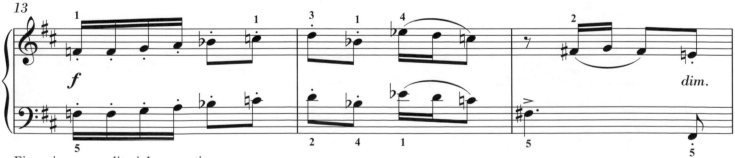

Fingerings are editorial suggestions.

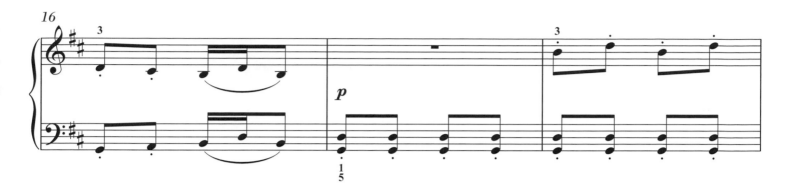

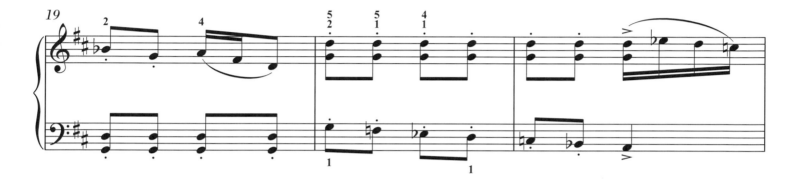

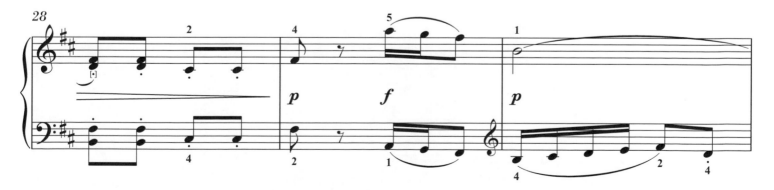

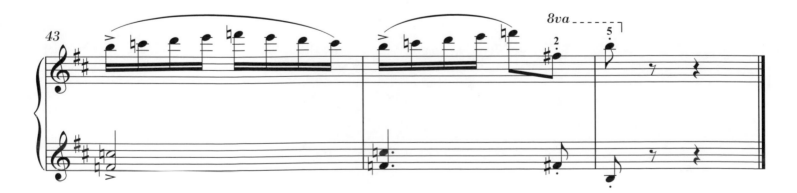

# Sonatina

from *30 Pieces for Children*

Dmitri Kabalevsky
Op. 27, No. 18

**Allegretto [♩ = c. 132]**

Fingerings are editorial suggestions.

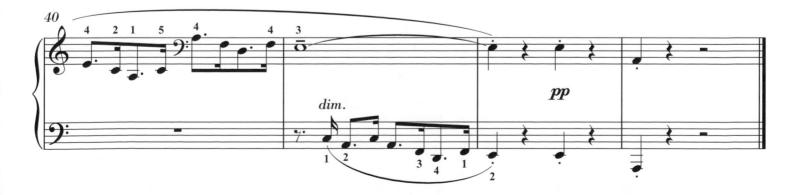